THE ROLLING STONES

THE ROLLING STONES IN EUROPE

Photographs by Philip Kamin
Text by James Karnbach

Beaufort Books

New York   Toronto

Library of Congress Cataloging in Publication Data
Main entry under title:
The Rolling Stones in Europe.
1. Rolling Stones. 2. Rock musicians — England — Interviews.
I. Rolling Stones. II. Kamin, Philip. III. Karnbach, James.
ML421.R647 1983   784.5′4′00922 [B] 83-2646
ISBN 0-8253-0152-1 (pbk.)

Published in the United States by
Beaufort Books
9 East 40th Street
New York, New York
10016

First Edition
10 9 8 7 6 5 4 3 2 1

Printed and bound in Canada

Design/Maher & Murtagh

ACKNOWLEDGMENTS

For Al and Terry.

I would like to thank the following for their help and cooperation: Art Collins, Alvenia Bridges, Paul Wasserman, Gordon Bennett, Cathy, Pam, Jane Rose, Greg Gadson, Bob Bender, Jonathan Smeeton, Spot, the Stones and Gene Barge, Joe Seabrook, Mick Brigden, Robert Bonneville, Jim Rooney, Evelyn Watt.

To my assistant, Bruce Evans, my assistant in Europe, Brad Simon, and travel coordinator Cathy Spanton, my vote of appreciation.

I would also like to thank Allan Stokell, C.J. Morgan and Don Hood at Positive Images, Toronto; Doug Paddey, Marty Ingles and Gary Beck at Canon Cameras of Canada; Steve Coomber at Ilford Films; Bob, Glen and Skip at Steichenlab, Toronto. And Creative Color, Frankfurt, Germany — special thanks to Franz and Bert.

P.K.

Very special thanks to my left-hand gal, Ms. Tracey Birnhak, for her support, knowledge and effort. I would also like to thank the following people for being so great and helpful, and who shared in the development of this book: Mindy Burton, Phyllis Rosney, Sherry Lutz, Bill German, Daniel Gardin, Jimmy Paulo, Ricky Ebberheart, Beggar's Banquet Fanzine, Ron Furmanek, Susan Crane, Philip Kamin, The Karnbach family, Ethel Karnbach, James Karnbach Sr., Alan Lysaght and David Pritchard at The Sonic Workshop, Toronto, Ron Wood, Joseph Kovacs.

J.K.

THE
ROLLING
STONES

Leeds, England

STILL LIFE
A PORTRAIT OF
THE ROLLING STONES ON TOUR

London, June 1, 1982. It must be my imagination running away with me. I can't believe The Rolling Stones are coming back. Europeans are once again blessed and about to be mesmerized, stormed and shattered by the legendary rock quintet from England. Rumors had been floating around for months—first tour on, then tour off—but confirmation finally came on April 18th, 1982, when Mick officially announced the European tour to the press at the fashionable London discoteque, Le Beat Route. Mick fed the press long awaited information: the tour would open June 4th, 1982 at Feyernoord Stadium in Rotterdam, Holland. Ironically, the tickets for that particular show were already sold out by the day of the conference. A third show was added to satisfy the overwhelming demand. June 2nd became the new opening date. Mick then went to Paris and Munich to make similar announcements about opening dates and the itinerary of the tour.

The Rolling Stones began rehearsing for the mammoth tour in early May at Shepperton Studios, London, England. The band had a long list of new songs to choose from for their show; it has been six years and five albums since their last tour of Europe. Songs were chosen, dropped, picked again and then rehearsed but, as the tour got closer, the Stones decided to make the 1982 European tour an extension of the 1981 American tour. The set from the American tour was perfected like a fine art, and the band feels that European fans will be getting the best possible performance, an even better show than that witnessed by their American fans.

The Stones rehearsed day and night. Meanwhile, the press and fans made their plans to converge on Rotterdam for the opening dates. But the Stones felt a warm-up was needed (they had performed at Sir Morgan's Cove in Worcester, Mass. before opening the '81 U.S. tour in Philadelphia) and consequently decided to do some unannounced shows in Scotland. They did three to be exact. The first show was in Aberdeen on May 26th, followed by Glasgow on the 27th, and then Edinburgh on the 28th. The shows went off well because the small theaters that they played allowed the band to recapture a sense of intimacy with their fans, which is virtually impossible in the large stadiums that the magnitude of their following requires them to play.

Press and fans alike were thrown for a loop. The Stones surprised everyone. The shows were so secretive and executed so swiftly and silently that news of them was outdated by the time the press found out. All the fans could hope for was a review of the shows. And, just when everyone thought they had missed the last surprise, The Rolling Stones snuck into a sleepy London town on May 31st to play a set at the famous 100 Club, with its seating capacity of 350 to 400 maximum. This morning many fans kicked themselves for missing the rare, once-in-a-lifetime chance to catch the Stones in such a small venue.

When the Stones appeared at the 100 Club, the loose and relaxed atmosphere led to an impromptu set variation from the shows done in Scotland. Without an introduction, the band stepped onstage and opened the set with *Chantilly Lace*. The usual opening number, *Under My Thumb*, forfeited its premier position. The audience at the 100 Club was allowed the rare privilege of witnessing the finesse that brought The Rolling Stones their world acclaim at close quarters.

The time has come for the tour to begin, and *Still Life* has been released in Europe, but not in America. The L.P. was even sold at the concession stands at the surprise shows in Scotland. The set, rehearsed and dress rehearsed before a live audience, is ready to move out. The press has hounded the entourage consisting of Bill Graham and his company, Raindrop Productions, Alan Dunn (logistics), Jim JC Callahan (head of security), a 130-man crew, eight trucks (Edwin & Shirley & Co.), four stages, and the band of Rolling Stones, who are ready to cut a concert path through Europe the likes of which has never before been witnessed here.

Rotterdam, June 2, 1982. Feyernoord Stadium. Spring has not yet drawn to a close, but it feels as though summer is already here. The temperature has risen to about eighty-five or ninety degrees, and some 50,000 fans stand shoulder-to-shoulder, waving and clapping in anticipation. All their attention is focused on the sixty-five-foot wide stage and the 150-foot-high curtains which are covered with a pastel "still life" of a guitar, car, and saxophone, in a style reminiscent of Art Deco. It was designed by artist Kazuhide Yamazaki for both the American and European tours.

George Thorogood, who opened for the Stones on a number of shows on the 1981 U.S. tour, is the opening act in Holland. He has his fans in Europe, too. His musical roots and style stem from the rock'n'roller who influenced Keith Richards so much, Chuck Berry. Thorogood's brand of rock'n'roll fits perfectly with the sheer exuberance of the audience.

The Boston-based J. Geils Band, another true hard rock'n'roll band, with similar roots to the Stones, follows George Thorogood. They too are warmly received by The Rolling Stones-starved fans of Rotterdam. From the conclusion of the J. Geils set, it takes an hour to reset the stage for the entrance of the Stones.

The crowd waits as patiently as a crowd can wait, but they are tipped off by the Stones' intro, *Take The "A" Train*, the classic Duke Ellington composition which sets the crowd ablaze at Feyernoord Stadium. The so anxiously awaited words finally hit the ears of the attentive fans—"Ladies and gentlemen, please welcome The Rolling Stones." Still hard to believe it is true, the opening chords of *Under My Thumb* blast out across the stadium field like a wave of cool water streaming over the audience.

Jagger, the center of attraction as usual, works the crowd like an old pro to both his and the band's best advantage. As if the audience has been told to watch the bouncing ball, the fans watch the leaps and bounds of Jumpin' Jack Jagger. Jagger howls out the opening lines of *Under My Thumb*. Then, direct from center stage, Richards and Wood come down to greet the audience. Surrounding Jagger like the covers of a book, Wood on the left and Richards on the right, they hold together the text of their music. It becomes not merely words behind the pen in the mind of the artist, but the style in which they are contained. Poetry is displayed with each note they play. Movement and *meaning* are defined with the rhythm and beat punctuating each note. The steady flow of the beat comes from the least-known face of the band, Charlie Watts, half hidden behind his drum kit. Bass player Bill Wyman, who usually seldom moved during a performance in the past, is now on the prowl. Bill has put out a couple of solo projects that have been quite successful in Europe, and when he is introduced later in the show, he is given a well-rounded greeting from all the fans. On keyboards, an original member of The Rolling Stones, Ian Stewart, is accompanied by Mr. Chuck Leavell, keyboard player for the Allman Brothers. Chuck made an earlier cameo appearance with the Stones on the 1981 tour in Atlanta, Georgia at the Fox Theater.

It is these special ingredients which make up the recipe to satisfy the starving Stones' fans of Europe. The audience is hot, and The Stones are cooking. *Under My Thumb,* a Jagger-Richard composition written in 1965, was never released as a single, yet met with the raves of a single, making it *the* classic tune with which to open the show. It is a song which reflects the Stones probably at their most decadent, as far as the press and parents see them.

The audience, 50,000 fans, mass force and power, is now controlled by the Fabulous Five. But it is all Mick Jagger in the way they respond for the next two hours. Jagger is sporting red-and-white striped trousers, and a flowered, short-sleeved Hawaiian shirt. He is a colorful sight on the stage. Dressed in his usual free-form style, Mick's Glimmer Twin mate sports a ripped T-shirt with the word "Heaven" across it, and a pair of jeans.

Apart, both Mick and Keith have a certain awesome quality which gives each their own identity, but when the two appear together onstage the chemical reaction is explosive, and they play off each other, which fulfils their own needs and makes the Stones, the Stones.

Paris, France

After the last note of *Under My Thumb* sounds, the audience goes into a mass frenzy, as if the opening ovation has still not died down. Only a few seconds pass before Keith hammers out the opening riffs to *When The Whip Comes Down*. Timing is all a part of the act; it is tight and keeps it all together. *When The Whip Comes Down* has never been played in Europe, and the audience responds accordingly, like a child given a gift. It has been on European turntables for four years, and now it is being seen and heard live— what a sweet treat. Its rhythm belts the crowd with the blow it has been so eagerly awaiting. Mick is very elusive on the stage, running down the right ramp with his guitar in hand. As Mick smiles and peers out at the audience, he shakes his hips rhythmically to the tempo of the tune.

Jagger is a singer-songwriter and dancer. He is branded "The Wizard of Rock," pulling out new tricks at each show. It is so hot that Mick's shirt is already soaking wet. To be so in control and the focus of so many peering eyes, most anyone would end up losing all of their composure, but not Mick. He has been through it all, and he knows what the crowd likes and gives them what they want. As Mick comes up to the edge of the ramp (stage right), the crowd in that part of the stadium goes crazy. At first Mick toys with them a little, acting as if he does not notice the high intensity level that he's creating, and he looks out even further into the audience which incites that section's frenzied response even more. Then, finally, like a gentle brush stroke on a canvas, Mick peers into the ranting crowd below, but only for a few seconds before the aloof Mr. Jagger is heading back to the center of the stage.

The band plays loud and clear, and the response is great. Ron Wood, ex-Faces and Jeff Beck Group member, a wild and happy-go-lucky fellow onstage, is always kidding around with the crowd or the band, and Rotterdam is no exception. With a cigarette dangling from his mouth, Woody goes to the left of the stage, pausing every now and then to peer down at the crowd and carry on short conversations with the audience. At one particular moment a sign is held up which says "We Love Ron Wood." Wood sees it, acts surprised, waves to his adoring fans, and throws them a big kiss. Woody then continues his jolly way down the ramp to the very end where he then, like a gangster, sprays the audience with lead riffs. The expression on his face is as though he is in pain, but actually it is the reflection of the feeling that comes out of his music.

Woody then retreats back to home base to join Keith Richards with back-up vocals to *When The Whip Comes Down*. As the song winds down, the ovation once again becomes deafening. Mick thanks the audience for coming to the show, steps back, grabs a can of soda, and takes a couple of swigs. Keith fine-tunes his guitar. Bill adjusts his bass amp. Jagger steps up to the microphone and asks the audience if they would like to spend the night together. Everyone knows it is the cue for the next tune, *Let's Spend The Night Together*, the 1967 single with which the Stones again placed themselves in the Top 10 of the most degenerate bands in the opinion of parents of the day. The sexually suggestive song became a hit with limited air play due to the nature of the material. Again the Stones are digging into their past, but *Let's Spend The Night Together* has been an anthem for another generation. It becomes more and more evident that the fans need the Stones now more than ever, as will be the case with all of Europe.

The set runs along smoothly: after *Let's Spend The Night Together* comes *Shattered*, *Neighbors*, *Black Limousine*, and the old Temptations' song, *Just My Imagination*. Next comes *20 Flight Rock*, an old Eddy Cochran tune; *Going To A Go-Go*, a Smokey Robinson & The Miracles number; and *Chantilly Lace*, a song recorded by the Big Bopper. The cover tunes (songs written and performed by other artists first) are paced rather quickly, without much let-up in between songs, and the band maintains the pace, moving into *Let Me Go* as the next number. The Stones have virtually exhausted the audience with a sort of musical bearhug. *Let Me Go* is a track from the album *Emotional Rescue*. This song, however, does not receive as enthusiastic a response as its predecessor. It is not as familiar a tune, so the band gives the fans a chance to cool down, just a little. The Stones follow with *You Can't Always Get What You Want*, and after the song concludes, Mick introduces the members of the band. Last to be introduced is Keith Richards. Mick tells the audience Richards is going to sing the next tune: "And Keith is gonna sing a *Little T & A* for you now." On cue, a tremendous riff screams out. Keith stands center stage as Jagger goes backstage to dry off and change his shirt, while his twin holds the rock'n'roll fort together. *Little T & A* is a hard driving, full-force song with a great steady beat. Keith is joined by Woody for some two-part harmony, and together they look barbaric. *Little T & A* riffs let it be known why some people call Keith the "Human Riff." It is a true Keith Richards' song. The audience is once again up on its feet, dancing.

When *Little T & A* ends, Mick comes out from behind the amps and goes to the mike to thank Keith. No sooner is Mick finished thanking Keith, than the opening bars to *Tumblin' Dice* blare out. The audience loves it, and the swirling mass of faces are gleaming with joy. *She's So Cold* and *Hang Fire* follow. They are spin-off singles from *Emotional Rescue* and *Tattoo You*, and fit together perfectly. Everyone is now wild in Feyernoord; everyone is interested in only one thing—the Stones. It is here that the Stones throw the rock'n'roll net over the audience, for the next six tunes are the tunes that had literally wiped out millions of fans in the U.S. in 1981. Europeans were now the next to be devoured.

Miss You is the first of the slaughterhouse six. It is the entrapment tune. A frenzy starts; no one is thinking about what time it is or where their friends are now. All outside thoughts are thoroughly banished. *Miss You* has them under its spell. Right after *Miss You* comes *Honky Tonk Woman*, and everyone is jumping, cheering, and singing along to those all-too-familiar lyrics. *Brown Sugar* follows and hearts are beating faster and faster. Everyone in the audience is sweating profusely. The Stones are all over the stage—Bill is up toward the front, Keith and Woody are all the way over to the right ramp, and Mick is running everywhere, from left to right and back again. Bobby Keys and Gene Barge are playing sax. Charlie Watts has been keeping the flow going, and he provides the kick the band needs. It's as Keith says of the Stones' drummer, "If Charlie don't get into it, then I haven't written something that the Stones can get a groove going on." Charlie hides behind the drums, ever so slightly out of view. If this rock'n'roll quintet were gangsters, Charlie would be the one who would drive the getaway car. Keith and Woody would carry the violin cases, while Bill would stand flipping coins. Jagger would be the one who does all the talking.

Start Me Up is next, which is rather ironic because if this audience is not worked up by this time, they would have been declared clinically dead. Feyernoord is a madhouse now. What happens in the stadium at first view could be described as a riot, but the people are not rioting, they are cheering, jumping, and singing and having a great time. They are not harming anyone. It is just good old rock'n' roll the way it should be. The Stones are gladiators, and it is now time to slay the audience. *Jumpin' Jack Flash* is the song that slays the fans. Everybody goes wild. They are peaking.

Jumping' Jack Flash ends, and the Stones thank everyone for coming, and George Thorogood and the J. Geils Band for their great sets, and then they leave the stage. Feyernoord now sounds like a union rally with the thunder of hands clapping and chants of "We want the Stones." After a few minutes the curtains open, and once more it is the Stones onstage to give and perform *Satisfaction*. Whatever energy the audience has saved up to help themselves out of the stadium, is being used up now. Jagger looks refreshed, and has as much vigor as when he first stepped out on the stage two hours earlier. Keith and Woody are the slavedrivers with riffs and leads that are leaving permanent lacerations on the memories of all the fans present. The way the audience is singing every verse with Mick, one would think that *Satisfaction* is the national anthem of Holland. It is over all too soon, as the last notes die away. The band is out of the stadium in no time, and the fans cannot believe what a great concert they've just witnessed.

The Stones have left a very satisfied and exhausted crowd, but wait—they are not finished yet. This is only the first show of three in this stadium in Rotterdam. Not only that, but it is the first city of a fifty-three-day tour. The Stones are great, and Rotterdam knows it. Oh, and Happy Birthday, Charlie.

Paris, June 13, 1982. The Rolling Stones' visit to Paris includes two concerts at the Hippodrome. The Hippodrome is the largest venue in Paris for a concert, with a capacity of 45,000. For two days in mid-June, it is the meeting place for a combined 90,000 Rolling Stones' fans. The Paris audience is rather different from other European crowds; the generally younger audience is comprised of more males than females. As Richards says, "The audiences in Europe change from country to country. In France it's really 80 percent boys. Chicks don't go to rock and roll shows in France. It's not chic or whatever."

The Stones are not unfamiliar faces in Paris, even though it has been six years since their last concert here. Paris has been home for the Stones' studio sessions, as their last three studio albums have been recorded at EMI Pathe Marconi Studios.

The Stones make the Warwick Hotel their home for their stay in Paris. Unlike the situation in the States, European fans, Parisians for example, do not hang around in the front of the hotel or try to sneak in and make a ruckus. Security for the Stones has always been notoriously tight, but over here fan pressure is less intense and security is a little more lax.

Paris is the mecca for well-known personalities, and when a big event occurs, you can bet they're going to show up. Stones' concerts are big events, and, as expected, backstage is the watering hole for some big names. One face in the crowd is director Roman Polanski. But backstage is not what it is all about; onstage is where the real action happens.

George Thorogood opens the concert. George proves he is a true rock'n'roller, and plays with all his heart and real feeling, which delights the audience.

The next band to appear is the J. Geils Band. They are the official opening act for the Stones' European tour. During the show, lead singer Peter Wolf slips and hits his head on the stage. After finishing the set, he is rushed to hospital, but the examination reveals no injury, and he is able to perform at the next day's show.

The chants grow louder and louder; Paris wants The Rolling Stones. The stage curtains are drawn closed as a huge cheer erupts from the field. Duke Ellington's *Take The "A" Train* plays, and then they are here—"Mesdames et messieurs, Les Rolling Stones." It is bedlam. People jump over one another, and hands and arms are flung into the air. People scream and cheer at the top of their lungs. They are seeing The Rolling Stones.

The Stones have always had a way of picking the most energetic tunes to open a show. The driving energy of *Under My Thumb* raises the excitement level of the Parisian audience,

Rotterdam, Netherlands

and with the music that level is maintained throughout the show.

The Stones have played everywhere and under all circumstances. Their strength is proved every time they step onstage. When the Stones start *Shattered*, the Parisian audience is shattered; the fans know what it is all about—the long tough road today. The Rolling Stones put it all out, and the fans try to keep pace. *Shattered* may be a song about New York City, but it has the style that fits all cities, and Paris is a perfect example. The audience dances and sings along, while Jagger prances about and swivels his hips, teasing the audience. He spreads himself all over the

stage, which causes havoc wherever he goes. The tempo is hot, and the audience has been taken over by the mighty Jagger. The Stones' set is strong, and they let the blues influence that is always with them come through. *Black Limousine*, the traditional blues tune, allows the audience to see the lift it gives the Stones every time they play it. The crowd is treated to the blues played by fine bluesmen in the style that has molded the band into what the crowd sees now. Wood and Richards display some fine guitar playing, and the slower pace helps the audience to calm down and regain its composure.

But that doesn't last too long. When the Stones start *Going To A Go-Go*, everyone is once again up on their feet. The dancing tune lifts the audience right back into a party mood. The Rolling Stones give the Parisian fans the music that they need to keep them going. The rest of the set brings the audience to the brink of complete exhaustion. The Stones carry their fans to the top, and then give them the "satisfaction" which they had come to get.

London, June 25, 1982. When the Stones arrive to play London, there is a major public transportation (tube) and railroad strike. Most large events are cancelled, or, if not, have a very poor turnout. But this is not holding true for The Rolling Stones. Although Wembley Stadium is some thirty miles from central London, the people are obviously not going to miss seeing the band, even if they have to walk the distance. Wembley can hold 70,000, and both shows are sold out.

While backstage usually sports an array of stars, backstage at Wembley has the real "personal" stars of the Stones. Each of the Stones has members of his family backstage; it is a moving get-together. Mick is with his parents, and Keith is with his parents too, as well as his son Marlon and daughter "Dandelion."

The show will be taped by the Stones' mobile unit for full twenty-four track audio recording and video hook-up for the giant projectors above the stage. The Stones feel right at home—and the show is extra special—for the parents, videotaping, and especially for the fans who have made the extra effort to get to the show.

Take The "A" Train starts, and it is frenzy time all over again. It seems to be contagious; whenever the Stones set foot onstage, no matter where in the entire world, the results are the same. It seems to be universal therapy for every fan to let out energy and jump, scream, and dance, and just have a great time. It is jam-packed up front, wall-to-wall people. Toward the back of the field, it is a huge dance floor with people dancing in groups, by themselves, or with whomever is near.

The set is running in fine gear; *Neighbors* receives an excellent response. The audience is dazed and overwhelmed. Jagger struts to the end of the ramps, weaving back and forth. The audience mimics his movements. He winks to someone in the audience and throws a big kiss, then runs back to his comrades of rock and roll. One of the most impressive moments during the set occurs when Mick leads the 70,000 fans in the chant of "You Can't Always Get What You Want." It seems to reflect the struggle everyone had in finding means of getting to the show. Mick is up to his old antics, toying with the fans. Mick loves to tease, and the audience plays right into his hands. He runs up the ramps, stops to look at the audience as if to say, "Come on up and join me," but as quick as a flash he moves away, leaving the ecstatic, heart-beating fans all alone. Mick and the boys are really cooking; the force is with them, and Wembley is rocking. A big screen above the stage shows good close-ups of the band. People way in the back of the stadium get to see, larger-than-life the amazing facial expressions that Jagger is famous for.

The Stones have the place peaking toward the end of the set. When *Start Me Up* begins, everyone in the stadium is up on their feet. The song has a drive that, when performed live, has to be seen to be believed. The song turns even the mellowest fan into a raving, dancing machine. All of Wembley is knocked senseless. The encore, *Satisfaction*, is played real tight and loud. It is a great way to end a fantastic show—and the Stones at the end come out for the first and only time onstage during the tour to give an encore bow before the 70,000 exhausted, bewildered, and satisfied fans.

Frankfurt, June 29, 1982. The Rolling Stones have ten shows scheduled for Germany on the 1982 tour, more than in any other country, including England. Rolling Stones' fans in Germany are truly loyal, and appreciate the rock'n'roll excellence, style and charisma of the Fantastic Five.

It's June 29. The Stones are in Frankfurt for three nights to play the smallest announced venue of the tour—Festhalle—which holds 12,000. Tickets outside are being scalped for four times the ticket price.

Inside Festhalle, the stage set-up is different from the one designed for their stadium shows. There are no large pastel-colored curtains strung across the stage. It is bare, with only amps and drums, but it still has the two ramps on either side which extend out into the audience. Without the colorful stage set, the only special effects will be the light show.

The acoustics in the hall are good, and it is considered one of the finest places in Frankfurt for a concert. Every seat allows a great view of the entire band.

The J. Geils Band warms up the audience for the appearance of the Stones. Their introduction carries the audience through the fifty-minute wait after J. Geils' set has finished, and when the Stones step onstage from the first note of *Under My Thumb* to the last note of *Satisfaction*, the tremendous intimacy of a small club is created. As in Scotland, the raw and awesome power of the band knocks out all of the fans present at Festhalle. *Under My Thumb* sounds real tight, and the Stones show Frankfurt the perfection of their art.

Mick feels right at home onstage. He is so close to the audience the fans could almost kiss him. He jumps down to the front of the stage and looks out beyond the first five rows of people. His eyes are wide open, his face tough and mean, but then, with a quick nod of his head, his smile becomes sweetly innocent yet seductive. Jagger catches and excites the crowd with the magic that has captured and excited so many of his fans. Jagger treats his fans to the unexpected and never fails to provoke the audience. Festhalle falls prey to his hypnotic antics.

The Rolling Stones' guitarists Keith Richards and Ron Wood treat the fans to the gutsy sound that rocks the house. The closeness of Festhalle convinces everyone present of the magnitude to which their music and performance dominate their lives. Every guitar lick is a message of feeling and care.

The Stones perform like never before, a truly magnificent effort. The fans respond by singing and dancing along with the band. Richards loves to play Germany: "In Germany they like to sort of get into a real jet-boot kind of march to each song. 'Everybody stamp your feet.' You don't ask them to clap their hands there 'cause they get it out like that. They like to march along."

About halfway through one of the shows, a fan gets so excited that he manages to get onstage. He is chased by security across the stage, passes the band, and leaps over a speaker monitor into the audience where he is swallowed up by the crowd. The incident does not affect the show; the Stones just keep going with their set. But toward the conclusion, things have almost gotten out of control. The audience is brought to such a fever pitch, it feels as though the house is going to crash down from the emotion. People are drenched as a result of the heat generated in the hall by the fans themselves, soaked by their own expenditure of emotion. Through *Brown Sugar*, with whatever energy they have left, everybody is jumping wildly to the music.

The band is everywhere onstage. Jagger crisscrosses back and forth as he weaves through the other band members, knitting them together with the suggestion of his actions. The fans are gasping for air from exhaustion. Their tongues are hanging out of their mouths by the time the Stones begin *Satisfaction*. By the time *Satisfaction* comes to a close, the hall has become one big sauna. The colorful balloons that are dropped on the audience and stage are bubbles of air floating down on a hall filled with emotion. As people leave Festhalle, they help each other to regain their composure and strength, which has been totally spent experiencing the incredible Rolling Stones.

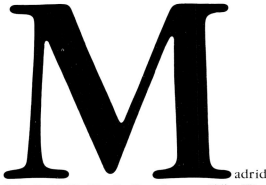

adrid, July 7, 1982. The Rolling Stones, "The World's Greatest Rock 'n' Roll Band," are playing second in terms of the interest of Madrid's local press only to the World Cup Soccer Championship. Madrid is hosting two events which electrify the city, and international attention is focused here. Everyone is talking soccer, but the Stones' impact is depicted by the sold-out show, while tickets are still available at the opening of the soccer match.

London, England

Barcelona was host to The Rolling Stones on their 1976 European tour, and they were so well received by the Spanish audience that Spain had to be included on the 1982 European tour. Today's torrential rains have done nothing to hinder the intense excitement which abounds in Madrid on this summer day. Soccer fans and rock enthusiasts have converged in Madrid from all the neighboring towns, and even other European countries. Hotels are completely booked, and have been for weeks. Calderon Stadium is SRO for the 70,000 fans waiting in the rain for the concert to begin.

The Stones seem to catapult themselves onstage. Their enthusiasm is electrifying; it's as if they want to show their appreciation for the loyal fans who have waited patiently in the rain for them to appear. Jagger shows that he is impressed with the turnout and audience's enthusiasm, and reflects it back to the crowd. The rain is forgotten as the Stones captivate all present. Nothing exists beyond the unfolding event.

Under My Thumb, Shattered, and *When*

The Whip Comes Down propel the audience into the rock frenzy created onstage. The crowd's reaction is one of sheer delight. Mick and Keith exhibit their true form — Mick swivelling his hips and Keith blasting the chords of creation. Rock music in its purest form.

Each song has its special set of fans and all songs are well received. But tonight, Madrid is given a treat. *Angie* is showcased for the first time on the 1982 European tour. As the tempo slows with the soft guitar riffs, Europe's biggest selling single is introduced as Mick steps to the mike and let's loose. *Angie* is, by overwhelming response, everyone's favorite tune. The fans are swept away. A calm settles over the stadium. The song seems to have brought joy to the crowd as the feeling of euphoria takes hold.

The audience is snapped out of the mood of *Angie* as the Stones launch their "Million Selling Singles Set." The set moves the audience to the climax which could only be fulfilled by *Satisfaction*.

Leeds, July 25, 1982. What has been one of the most successful European tours by any rock and roll band is closing in Leeds, England. The setting is Roundhay Park, and the crowd is the largest assembled for a single concert of the entire tour. There are 150,000 people here.

The Rolling Stones' Tour of Europe has been plagued by bad weather, but for the Leeds show the weather couldn't be better— an excellent day for an outdoor concert, and a wonderful way to end an unforgettable nine-week tour.

People began to arrive early in the morning to get ready for the day's events, and to get good positioning on the grounds to see the Stones on the mammoth stage. For this particular show, the Stones have combined the equipment from two of their four stage setups. There is twice as much equipment for the twice as many people than at any other single show. The Stones have truly gone all out for this final concert.

At five o'clock, the audience, treated to fine performances by Joe Jackson and J. Geils, is waiting for the real reason that brought them here—The Rolling Stones. As the pink drapes are drawn shut, the crowd becomes ecstatic. The once again popular *Take The "A" Train* kicks off the sparks to the pulsating beat of *Under My Thumb*. Mick Jagger, wearing a red jacket with red-and-white striped pants, dances down the stage platform. His jumping and acrobatic acts are all so perfect. His stage antics and teasing are all on cue. He knows how to use his body, and he uses it well. But there is the sense that Mick and the band know that this is the end of the tour, and they are not scheduled to play somewhere tomorrow or for a while. The Leeds show has a special feeling to it. The five-member family is going to go their separate ways, but for this family the best way to deal with their temporary separation is to perform their last show in overdrive, to make it the best dance-party-concert they can to remind them of the force which has kept the nucleus of this family together for the previous nine weeks.

The set runs about the same as the other previous shows in London. *Let's Spend The Night Together* receives a tremendous response from the audience. It brings everyone to their feet, dancing. The music is pulling everybody in. Closer to the stage, and to the Stones' performance, people want to party, dance even harder, and sing along. This number urges the crowd first to near hysteria, then to total hysteria.

Keith Richards never lets up. His driving riffs push the band to generate more and more energy through each song. Keith shows no wear and tear from the tour, but rather has a more healthy look about him, an indication he is enjoying himself. Keith keeps looking back and forth, from Jagger to Wood, as if to signal how great playing is, and what a feeling it is to have so many people enjoying themselves from the music you're playing.

During the set Mick stops to put on a hat. He takes it off and pretends to toss it out into the audience just to tease them a little. Keith starts a slow riff and Mick steps up to the mike to sing *Time Is On My Side*. It is like that old black magic, the roots of a musical influence on the Stones, and a "memories" song for the audience. It is hard to believe that the Stones performed this song eighteen years ago, and even more incredible that they are once again performing it for their 150,000 fans gathered before them. Of all the tunes, it has to be the most sentimental song of the set by far—a conscience awareness song that will move people to reminisce about the past, what they were doing when this song came out or, if they were too young, their earliest recollections of hearing the tune.

The set is smooth. One of the most amazing sights occurs during *You Can't Alway Get What You Want*, when Jagger conducts the 150,000 fans in a sing-along. It is quite an awesome spectacle, a true indication of the power and control that Jagger and the Stones have on everyone. When the song ends the audience applauds not only the band but themselves, and Mick thanks them for joining in. Mick grabs ahold of the mike, and walks to the side of the stage to introduce the musicians. The band needs no formal introduction, but there could have been someone out there who had never before seen The Rolling Stones. The horn players are Bobby Keys and Gene

Barge, and Chuck Leavell is on keyboards; as the extended family members of the band, their introduction is fitting. Bill Wyman, Charlie Watts, and Ron Wood get their usual introductions. Mick never really introduces Keith but says, "Now Keith's gonna sing his song, a *Little T & A*." Keith steps to the front of the stage and takes the solo spotlight. He never has doubts or fears over his ability to perform, and his style and image are best reflected during this tune. Being the last gig of the tour, he makes it a really great showcase of what the Stones are all about. Its strong up-tempo beat and hard drive show what a rock'n'roll song is supposed to be.

The Stones add *Angie* to their set, which was not done in any of the previous shows in England on this tour. *Angie* is the Stones biggest selling single in Europe. England gives the band a great ovation for treating them to it. The song paces the set perfectly, and keeps the audience as up and ecstatic as they could be. The Stones then begin their pulverizing descent on the crowd with five tunes which massacre them. *Honky Tonk Woman* sets them up, *Brown Sugar* compacts them, *Start Me Up* renders them defenseless, *Jumping' Jack Flash* tears them up, and *Satisfaction* sweeps them away.

Then, it is all over. The last concert. The last gig of a truly exhausting tour. Roadies and stage crew break down the stage. Backstage there is a party for the band and crew. Everyone but Jagger hangs around—he left after a short while. Everyone is wishing everyone else well, and making plans to get together in the future.

July 26, 1982. The Rolling Stones' European Tour is over. It is also Mick Jagger's

birthday. The party thrown for Mick is relatively private, nothing as big as in previous years. Some friends are there—Ian Stewart, Alan Dunn, Kenney Jones (drummer for The Who), a few roadies, and some of the stage crew. Most of the Stones' touring party has gone their separate ways, back to their homes and to their families.

Bill Graham, who worked himself to exhaustion before the tour and then straight through it, has headed back to the U.S. to tie up loose ends for the up and coming Tom Petty tour. The preparation for that tour was done while Graham was on tour with the Stones. Bill Wyman has departed for his new home in London for a while. Charlie's schedule includes a little rest and relaxation. Keith is off to visit some old friends in Jamaica and to check on the new house he is having built there. Mick will stay in London for a while to visit with friends and family, and to plan new strategies for the Stones. Ron Wood has left for New York City to take his rest.

The Rolling Stones go their separate ways at the end of the tour, but this is not uncommon. They do it after every tour. The big questions in the minds of everyone involved are "Will they be back together again?" "Will they tour again?" "Are they bored with being The Rolling Stones after some twenty years?" Well, the best way to look at these questions is with a positive attitude.

The five people who make up The Rolling Stones are all musicians who enjoy what they do. Their past two tours, U.S. Tour 1981 and European Tour 1982, have been smash hits. To them, being musicians and playing the music they love is one thing, but turning so many people on by it and entertaining mass audiences with such success is the wind that keeps the Stones rolling. They have achieved the pinnacle of musical artistry, to turn people on by their music and their performances. The success of the American and European tours created so much momentum that perhaps the greatest rock'n'roll band in the world might not be able to stop rolling into another international tour. The forecast for a future tour would show as big a success. Future tours for The Stones are foreseeable, unless there is some strange turn of events. The outlook is positive.

The Stones—Mick, Keith and Woody—will gather in Paris in late autumn to review some old tapes and lay down some basic tracks for some new, recently written songs. They are arranging a comfortable time for everyone to get back into the studio to start production on the next L.P. so that it will be ready for release in the fall of 1983. As a result of the last two tours, the band has been a close-knit family for almost a year. Going into the studio now should show some of the good chemistry that continues to develop among them. They are hot right now, and they know how to keep the momentum going. The next studio L.P. should have a good feel to it, and possibly be one of the Stones' best L.P.'s ever.

The year 1983 marks the twentieth anniversary of The Rolling Stones' involvement in the music business. The Rolling Stones and their label, Rolling Stones Records, are planning some special events for this momentous accomplishment. Knowing the Stones, it can be guaranteed that this will be a wild and incredible celebration. The opening of the next Stones' film is also slated for 1983. It is titled, "Let's Spend the Night Together." Shot by Hal Ashby, the film contains footage shot at the Meadowlands Arena in New Jersey, U.S.A., and the Sun Dome Stadium in Phoenix, Arizona, U.S.A.

We can look forward to hearing and seeing plenty of The Rolling Stones in 1983, opening with the movie in February, an anniversary celebration in the summer, and a new studio L.P. expected for release in the fall. The band will carry the year along.

Paris, France

WELCOME TO THE ROLLING STONES

Lyons, France

Göteborg, Sweden ▶

Rotterdam, Netherlands

Cologne, Germany

Leeds, England

Frankfurt, Germany

Frankfurt, Germany

Frankfurt, Germany

Frankfurt, Germany

Frankfurt, Germany

Cologne, Germany

Madrid, Spain

Rotterdam, Netherlands

Madrid, Spain

Göteborg, Sweden

Göteborg, Sweden ▶

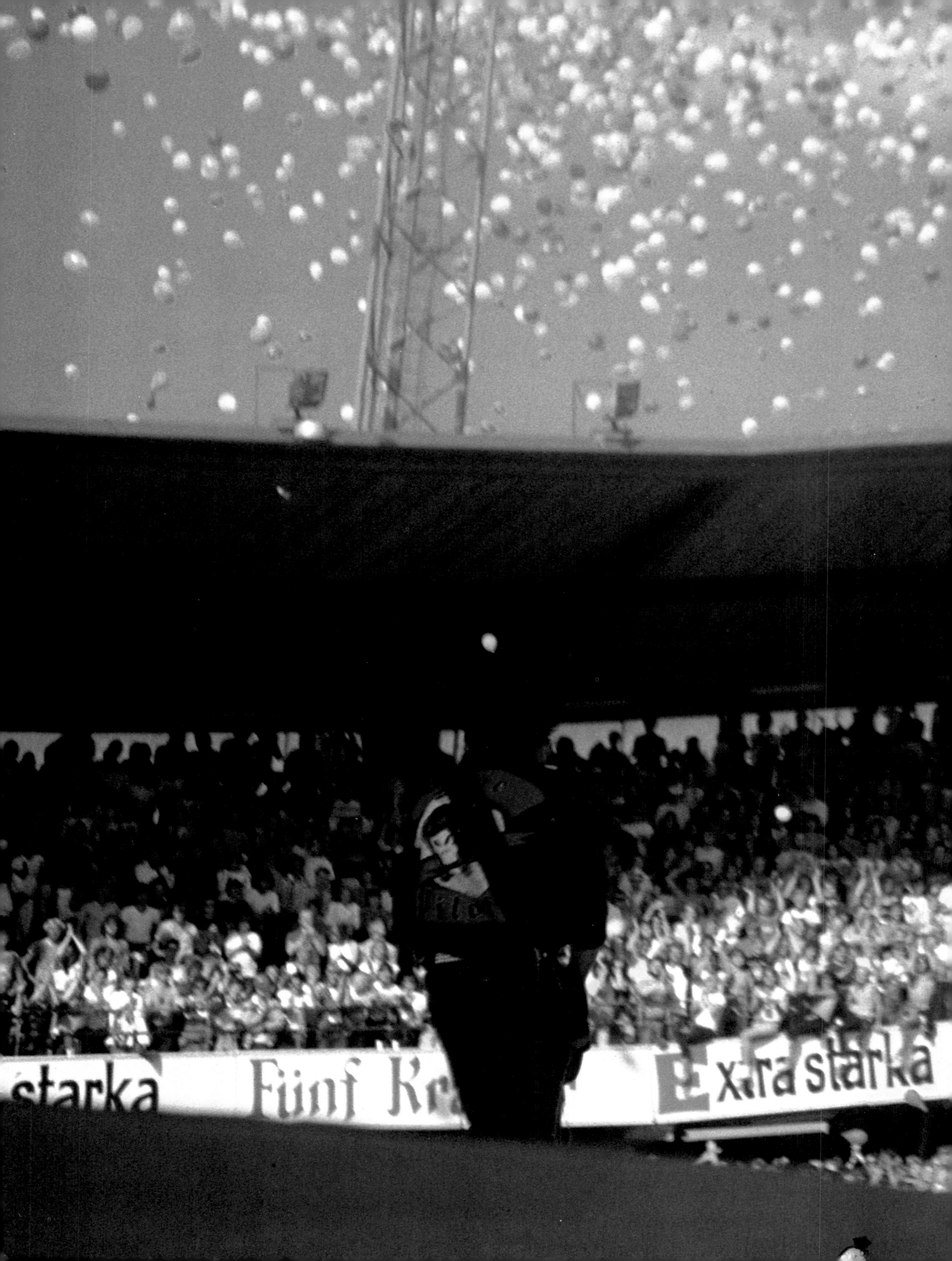
starka
Fünf
starka

Rotterdam, Netherlands

Rotterdam, Netherlands

Frankfurt, Germany ➤

Madrid, Spain ➤

Frankfurt, Germany

Frankfurt, Germany

Frankfurt, Germany

Leeds, England

Leeds, England

Leeds, England

Rotterdam, Netherlands

Rotterdam, Netherlands

Leeds, England

Leeds, England

▶

Frankfurt, Germany

Frankfurt, Germany

Lyons, France

Lyons, France

Lyons, France

Paris, France

Leeds, England

London, England

Cologne, Germany

Göteborg, Sweden

Göteborg, Sweden

Lyons, France

Madrid, Spain

Göteborg, Sweden ▶

London, England

London, England

Cologne, Germany

Rotterdam, Netherlands ►

Leeds, England ►

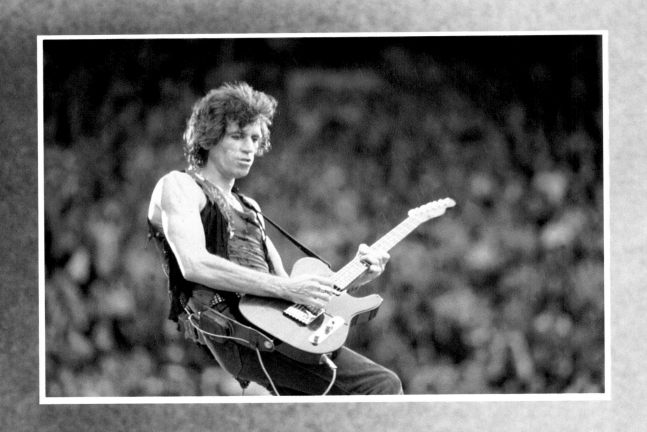

Leeds, England

Paris, France

Paris, France

Frankfurt, Germany

London, England

Cologne, Germany

Göteborg, Sweden

Frankfurt, Germany

Frankfurt, Germany

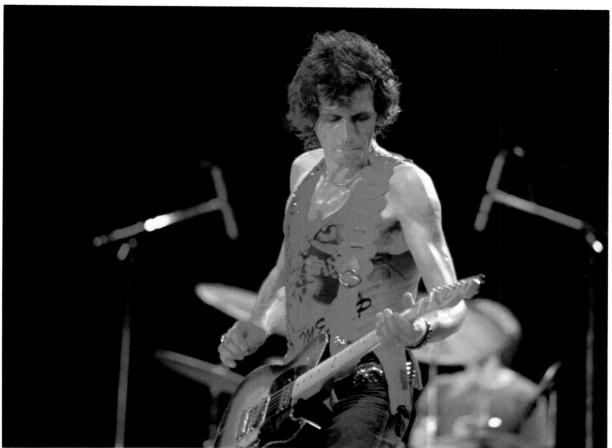

Frankfurt, Germany

Frankfurt, Germany

Madrid, Spain

Paris, France

Frankfurt, Germany

Frankfurt, Germany

Lyons, France

London, England ▶

Paris, France

Göteborg, Sweden

Leeds, England

Cologne, Germany

Leeds, England

Rotterdam, Netherlands

Göteborg, Sweden

Göteborg, Sweden

Rotterdam, Netherlands

◄ *Göteborg, Sweden*

Frankfurt, Germany

Madrid, Spain

Rotterdam, Netherlands

Paris, France

Göteborg, Sweden

Cologne, Germany

Cologne, Germany

Cologne, Germany

Cologne, Germany

Cologne, Germany

Rotterdam, Netherlands

Lyons, France

Paris, France

Frankfurt, Germany

Frankfurt, Germany

Paris, France

London, England

Leeds, England

London, England

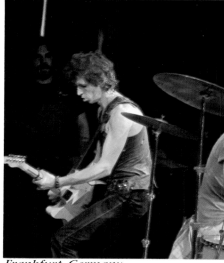

Frankfurt, Germany

Rotterdam, Netherlands

Göteborg, Sweden

Paris, France

Göteborg, Sweden

Paris, France

London, England ►

Leeds, England ►

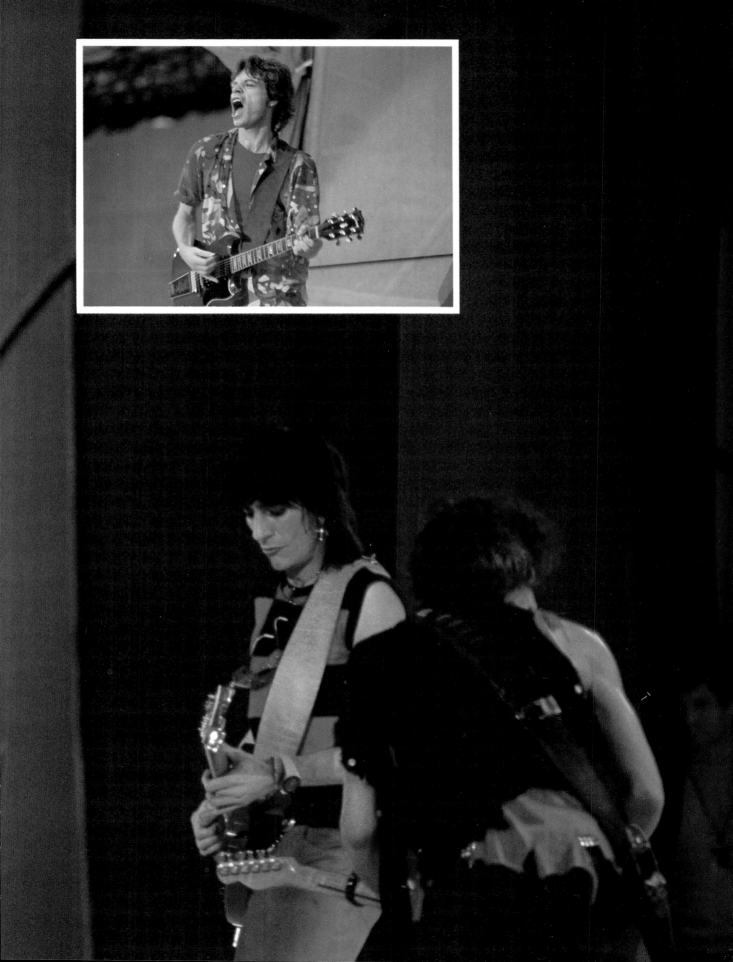

Lyons, France

Lyons, France ►

Göteborg, Sweden

Paris, France

Rotterdam, Netherlands

Lyons, France

Frankfurt, Germany

Rotterdam, Netherlands

London, England

Frankfurt, Germany

Lyons, France

Leeds, England

Rotterdam, Netherlands

London, England

Göteborg, Sweden ►

Frankfurt, Germany

Göteborg, Sweden

Lyons, France ►

AN INTERVIEW WITH RON WOOD

On the road and then some.

Q: Did you enjoy the 1982 European tour?

A: Yeah, quite well in fact. We were really psyched up for it. The band just finished the U.S. tour, so we were primed for Europe. We played much bigger places in Europe *this* tour, than on previous ones.

Q: What are the differences between touring in the U.S. as opposed to touring in Europe, specifically: financially, travel-wise, press coverage, food and security?

A: *Financially:* We make much more money touring the U.S. than Europe. You just about break even there.
Travel: Well, in the U.S. you don't have customs problems every time you go to a different state, but in Europe there's customs everywhere you go. And each country has different currency, so you're constantly changing it. And language changes in various countries; in the U.S. they all speak English.
Press: We receive *much* more publicity in the U.S. than in Europe.
Food: When touring the U.S., food is readily available twenty-four hours a day, but in Europe it's rarely accessible after certain hours.
Security: About the same in both areas, although we are not bothered as much by the fans in Europe.

Q: Can you talk about playing in other cities?—specifically: Rotterdam, Paris, Frankfurt, London, Göteborg and Madrid.

A: Rotterdam was really incredible! I believe it was the first big venue on the '82 tour. I remember it was really hot that day, and the fans were really great.
Paris: Ah yes. We played in a horse jumping field with all the hedges about four feet high for the horses to jump over. We had some problems with the sound that day. "Telephone" played on one of those shows.
Frankfurt: The fans there are really wild—jumping and cheering—I remember some guy jumped onto the stage, and when security went after him, he just dove off the stage right into the audience.
London: Everybody was there! All Stones' relatives, including Mick's mom and dad. And friends—John Entwistle, John McEnroe, Vitas Gerulaitis. It was really great! We has lots of fun there.
Göteborg: A great show! We played extremely well there. The crowd was really up for the show—they wouldn't let up for a minute. Keith slipped and fell during *Beast Of Burden*. I looked over and there he was on the floor!
Madrid: There was when the world cup tournament was on, and we were backstage watching the game. I remember it rained an awful lot—it was the worst rainstorm we ever played in.

Q: What was the funniest thing that happened on the European tour?

A: I remember Keith slipping on a frankfurter onstage in Frankfurt—oh wait—that may have been the '76 tour! Oh well! It was rather funny, whenever it was.

Q: How was traveling different in Europe on this tour, as opposed to the previous tours there?

A: In '82 we flew everywhere, while in '76 we flew, drove, took boats and rode buses. It was a lot quicker to go from one place to another, and we played to much larger crowds this tour than the '76 tour—and we finally made some money this tour!

Q: What are some of the good things that stand out in your mind about *this* European tour?

A: Lots of fun, good memories and beautiful scenery in every country.

Q: How's the new Stones' L.P. coming along?

A: Really good. We've got all new songs—it will be fantastic when it's released.

Q: What do you think of the new Hal Ashby film, "Let's Spend the Night Together"?

A: Haven't seen the final version yet. They have "Rocks Off" out in Europe. I heard some good reviews of it—look forward to seeing it soon.

Madrid, Spain

"26 x 5"
THE SONGS PERFORMED ON
THE 1982 TOUR OF EUROPE

he following is a list, song by song, of the set performed by The Rolling Stones on the 1982 European Tour. Each song is broken down as to where it was recorded, who it was written by, which L.P. it appeared on originally (only North American and British releases, the first two greatest hits L.P.'s, and the three greatest hits L.P.'s on Rolling Stones Records), and when, if ever, performed by the Stones live in concert in previous years.

(1) **Under My Thumb**
Written by Jagger/Richard
Recorded at R.C.A. Studios — Hollywood, Ca., March 1965.
Appears on L.P.'s: *Aftermath, Got Live If You Want It, Still Life*.
Performed Live: North American Tour 1966, British Tour 1966, European Tour 1967, North American Tour 1969, U.S. Tour 1981, European Tour 1982.

(2) **When The Whip Comes Down**
Written by Jagger/Richard
Recorded at Pathe Marconi Studios — Paris, France, May-August 1977.
Appears on L.P.'s: *Some Girls,* (live on) *Sucking In The Seventies*.
Performed Live: U.S. Tour 1978, Oshawa, Canada, 4/22/79, U.S. Tour 1981, European Tour 1982.

(3) **Shattered**
Written by Jagger/Richard
Recorded at Pathe Marconi Studios — Paris, France, May-August 1977.
Appears on L.P.'s: *Some Girls, Still Life*.
Performed Live: U.S. Tour 1978, Oshawa, Canada, 4/22/79, U.S. Tour 1981, European Tour 1982.

(4) **Let's Spend The Night Together**
Written by Jagger/Richard
Recorded at Olympic Studios — London, England, & R.C.A. Studios — Hollywood, Ca., Nov-Dec 1966.
Appears on L.P.'s: *Between The Buttons* (U.S. release only), *Flowers, Through The Past Darkly*.
Performed Live: European Tour 1967; Knebworth Show 8/21/76; El Mocambo Club, Toronto, Canada, March 4&5, 1977; U.S. Tour 1981; European Tour 1982.

(5) **Neighbors**
Written by Jagger/Richard
Recorded at Pathe Marconi Studios — Paris, France, & Atlantic Studios — New York, 1980-1981.
Appears on L.P.: *Tattoo You*.
Performed Live: U.S. Tour 1981, European Tour 1982.

(6) **Black Limousine**
Written by Jagger/Richard
Recorded at Pathe Marconi Studios — Paris, France, 1977.
Appears on L.P.: *Tattoo You*.
Performed Live: U.S. Tour 1981, European Tour 1982.

(7) **Just My Imagination**
Written by Whitfield-Strong
Recorded at Pathe Marconi Studios — Paris, France, May-August 1977.
Appears on L.P.'s: *Some Girls, Still Life*.
Performed Live: U.S. Tour 1978, Oshawa, Canada, 4/22/79, U.S. Tour 1981, European Tour 1982.

(8) **Twenty Flight Reck**
Written by Fairchild-Cochran
No known studio session.
Appears on L.P.: *Still Life*.
Performed Live: U.S. Tour 1981, European Tour 1982.

(9) **Going To A Go-Go**
Written by Robinson-Johnson-Moore-Rogers
No known studio session.
Appears on L.P.: *Still Life*.
Performed Live: U.S. Tour 1981, European Tour 1982.

(10) **Chantilly Lace**
Written by J.P. Richardson
No known studio session.
Appears only on European Tour 1982 bootleg L.P.'s.
Performed Live: European Tour 1982.

(11)Let Me Go
Written by Jagger/Richard
Recorded at Pathe Marconi Studios —
Paris, France, & Compass Point Studio
— Nassau, Bahamas, 1979-1980.
Appears on L.P.'s: *Emotional Rescue,
Still Life*.
Performed Live: U.S. Tour 1981,
European Tour 1982.

(12)Time Is On My Side
Written by Norman Meade
Recorded at Regent Sound — London,
England, February 1964, & I.B.C.
Studios — London, England, May 1964.
Appears on L.P.'s: *12 x 5, Rolling Stones
#2, High Tide & Green Grass,
Got Live If You Want It, Still Life*.
Performed Live: North American Tour
Oct-Nov 1964, European Tour 1965,
North American Tour 1965, Australian
Tour 1966, European Tour 1966, U.S.
Tour 1981, European Tour 1982.

(13)Beast Of Burden
Written by Jagger/Richard
Recorded at Pathe Marconi Studios —
Paris, France, 1977.
Appears on L.P.'s: *Some Girls, Sucking In
The Seventies*. Also, a live version from
Chicago concert 1981 was released
only as the "B" side to the 45 rpm
single, *Going To A Go-Go*.
Performed Live: U.S. Tour 1978, Oshawa,
Canada, 4/22/79, U.S. Tour 1981,
European Tour 1982.

(14)Let It Bleed
Written by Jagger/Richard
Recorded at Olympic Studios — London,
England, 1969.
Appears on L.P.: *Let It Bleed*.
Performed Live: U.S. Tour 1981,
European Tour 1982.

(15)You Can't Always Get What You Want
Written by Jagger/Richard
Recorded at Olympic Studios — London,
England, March-June 1968.
Appears on L.P.'s: *Let It Bleed, Love You
Live*.
Performed Live: Rolling Stones Rock 'n'
Roll Circus — December 12, 1968,
North American Tour 1972, European
Tour 1973, Far East Tour 1973, Los
Angeles Benefit Show for Nicaragua —
1/18/73, U.S. Tour 1978, U.S. Tour
1981, European Tour 1982.

(16)Little T & A
Written by Jagger/Richard
Recorded at Pathe Marconi Studios —
Paris, France, 1979-1980.
Appears on L.P.: *Tattoo You*.
Performed Live: U.S. Tour 1978,
European Tour 1982.

(17)Angie
Written by Jagger/Richard
Recorded at Dynamic Sound Studios —
Jamaica, West Indies, Nov 1972-
March 1973.
Appears on L.P.'s: *Goats Head Soup,
Made In The Shade, Time Waits For
No One*.
Performed Live: European Tour 1973;
North American Tour 1975; El
Mocambo Club, Toronto, Canada,
March 4 & 5, 1977; European Tour
1982.

(18)Tumbling Dice
Written by Jagger/Richard
Recorded at M.R.U. — Nellcote, France,
July-November 1971.
Appears on L.P.'s: *Exile On Main Street,
Love You Live, Made In The Shade*.
Performed Live: U.S. Tour 1971;
European Tour 1973; Benefit Show
for Nicaragua, Jan 18, 1973; North
American Tour 1975; European Tour
1976; El Mocambo Club, Toronto
March 4 & 5, 1977; U.S. Tour 1978;
U.S. Tour 1981; European Tour 1982.

(19)She's So Cold
Written by Jagger/Richard
Recorded at Compass Point Studios —
Nassau, Bahamas, 1979.
Appears on L.P.: *Emotional Rescue*.
Performed Live: U.S. Tour 1981,
European Tour 1982.

(20)Hang Fire
Written by Jagger/Richard
Recorded at Pathe Marconi Studios —
Paris, France, May-August 1977.
Appears on L.P.: *Tattoo You*.
Performed Live: U.S. Tour 1981,
European Tour 1982.

(21)Miss You
Written by Jagger/Richard
Recorded at Pathe Marconi Studios —
Paris, France, 1977.
Appears on L.P.: *Some Girls*.
Performed Live: U.S. Tour 1978, Oshawa,
Canada, Benefit Concert 1979,
U.S. Tour 1981, European Tour 1982.

(22) Honky Tonk Woman

Written by Jagger/Richard

Recorded at Olympic Studios — London, England, May 1969.

Appears on L.P.'s: *Through The Past Darkly, Get Yer Ya-Ya's Out!, Love You Live*.

Performed Live: Hyde Park Concert, London, England, July 5, 1969; North American Tour 1969; London Christmas Shows — Lyceum Theatre & Saville Theatre, December 14, 1969 & December 21, 1969; European Tour 1970; U.K. Tour 1971; European Tour 1973; Far East Tour 1973; North American Tour 1975; European Tour 1976; El Mocambo Club, Toronto, Canada, March 4 & 5, 1977; U.S. Tour 1978; U.S. Tour 1981; European Tour 1982.

(23) Brown Sugar

Written by Jagger/Richard

Recorded at Muscle Shoals Studios, Alabama, U.S.A, December 1969.

Appears on L.P.'s: *Sticky Fingers, Love You Live, Made In The Shade*.

Performed Live: Altamont Speedway, San Francisco, Ca. December 6, 1969; European Tour 1970; U.K. Tour 1970; North American Tour 1972; European Tour 1973; Benefit Concert for Nicaraguan Earthquake Victims, January 18, 1973; Far East Tour 1973; North American Tour 1975; European Tour 1976; El Mocambo Club, Toronto, Canada, March 4 & 5, 1977; U.S. Tour 1978; U.S. Tour 1981; European Tour 1982.

(24) Start Me Up

Written by Jagger/Richard

Recorded at Pathe Marconi Studios — Paris, France, May-August 1977.

Appears on L.P.'s: *Tattoo You, Still Life*.

Performed Live: U.S. Tour 1981, European Tour 1982.

(25) Jumpin' Jack Flash

Written by Jagger/Richard

Recorded at Olympic Studios — London, England, March 1968.

Appears on L.P.'s: *Through The Past Darkly, Get Yer Ya-Ya's Out!, Love You Live*.

Performed Live: Poll Winners Concert, May 11, 1968; Rolling Stones Rock'n' Roll Circus, London, England, December 12th, 1968; Hyde Park Concert, London, July 5, 1969; North American Tour 1969; Christmas Shows: Saville Theatre, December 14, 1969 & Lyceum Concert, December 21, 1969; European Tour 1970; U.K. Tour 1971; North American Tour 1972; European Tour 1973; Benefit Show for Nicaraguan Earthquake Victims, L.A. Ca., January 18, 1973; Far East Tour 1973; North American Tour 1975; European Tour 1976; El Mocambo Club, Toronto, Canada, March 4 & 5, 1977; U.S. Tour 1978; Benefit Concert for the Blind, Oshawa, Canada, April 22, 1979; U.S. Tour 1981; European Tour 1982.

(26) Satisfaction

Written by Jagger/Richard

Recorded at R.C.A. Studios — Hollywood, Ca., May 12, 13, 1965.

Appears on L.P.'s: *Out Of Our Heads* (U.S. version only), *High Tide & Green Grass, Got Live If You Want It, Still Life*.

Performed Live: North American Tour, Nov-Dec 1965; European Tour 1965; Far East Tour 1966; North American Tour 1966; European Tour 1966; European Tour 1967; Poll Winner Concert, Wembley, May 11, 1968; Hyde Park Concert, London, England, July 5, 1969; North American Tour 1969; Christmas Shows: Saville Theatre, December 14, 1969 & Lyceum Concert, December 21, 1969; European Tour 1970; U.K. Tour 1971; North American Tour 1972; European Tour 1973; North American Tour 1975; European Tour 1976; El Mocambo Club, Toronto, Canada, March 4 & 5, 1977; U.S. Tour 1978; U.S. Tour 1981; European Tour 1982.

QUESTIONS ABOUT THE STONES EVERYBODY ASKS

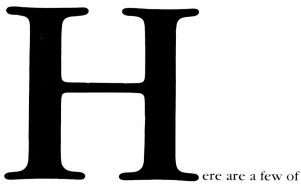

ere are a few of the "most asked" questions about the Stones' early days, their recording history, and touring.

When did the Stones first form as a group?

The Stones (Mick, Keith, Bill, Brian and Charlie) were first a group in very late 1962 and early 1963. Before then there were various changes in band personnel. Mick Avery of The Kinks and Dick Taylor of the Pretty Things were among early members of the band. The band was formed originally through an ad in a paper. Brian Jones was looking for musicians to form a blues band, and he gave Ian Stewart's telephone number to call.

When did the Stones first start recording?

The Stones first started recording as early as 1962, using a reel-to-reel tape recorder and an external mike in the garage of the homes of Dick Taylor and Mick Jagger. They did numbers like *Close Together, Soon Forgotten,* and *Can't Judge A Book By Its Cover*. These tapes are extremely rare and very crude.

The band did its first radio session in January, 1963 at Olympic Studios in London, England, with engineer and long-time friend Glyn Johns. They recorded five tunes: *Bright Lights Big City, Roadrunner, Honey What's Wrong, I Wanna Be Loved,* and *Diddley Daddy*. These tapes were submitted to various record companies but were turned down because the lead singer sounded "too colored." Their first record was recorded in Olympic Studios in May, 1963, which was *Come On,* a Chuck Berry song, and another version of Willy Dixon's tune, *I Wanna Be Loved*.

What was the first Jagger/Richard composition?

Although the first song the Stones came out with, with Jagger/Richard credited as writers, was *Tell Me* in 1964, before that they were penning tunes for other artists, mostly of the slow ballad type. The song released by George Bean titled *It Should Be You,* with the "B" side *Will You Be My Lover?,* released in January, 1964, was their very first.

Who was the Stones' first manager?

Their first manager was Giorgio Gomelsky, in 1963, when the Stones had residency at the famed Crawdaddy Club. In April of 1963, they were seen by Andrew Oldham and Eric Easton, and later signed a management contract with them. Later, in 1965, Allen Klein bought out Eric Easton and became a manager. In 1967, Andrew Oldham terminated his contract, and in 1970 Allen Klein no longer managed the Stones. Since then the Stones have overseen most of their business collectively, and have hired various people to handle certain business ventures.

Who is Nanker Phelge?

Nanker Phelge was a pseudonym used by the Stones when they wrote songs collectively.

What were the first appearances on television in Europe and the United States for The Rolling Stones?

The Stones appeared on the British television show "Thank Your Lucky Stars" on June 7, 1963 to promote the new single *Come On*. They showed up without jackets and were asked to wear suit jackets from the show's wardrobe room. In America, the Stones first appeared on the "Hollywood Palace" television show in June, 1964. There, host Dean Martin made the Stones the butt-end of his jokes. The Stones were not impressed with his humor.

Who plays lead guitar on Rolling Stones' records in the sixties?

Keith Richards played lead on most of the Stones' songs, while Brian Jones played rhythm guitar or experimented with new musical instruments for recordings. Brian Jones does play lead on *I Wanna Be Your Man* and *The Last Time*.

What films have The Rolling Stones in them?

The Stones were in "The T.A.M.I. Show" in 1964, and the Jean Luc Goddard film "One Plus One" in 1968, and also "Voices," another Goddard film. Also: "Popcorn," "Tonight Let's

Leeds, England

All Make Love In London" in 1967; "Gimmie Shelter," "Ladies & Gentlemen, The Rolling Stones," a 1972 concert film; and Hal Ashby's "Let's Spend The Night Together" aka "Rocks Off," and "Time Is On Our Side," plus others unreleased.

What has been the transition among band members of The Rolling Stones?

In 1963 there were six members, with keyboard player Ian Stewart being a front member. Andrew Oldham felt that "Stew's" rather straight image did not fit well with the long-haired, wild image the Stones seemed to portray, and it was decided to have Stew keep a low profile with the band. In June, 1969, Brian Jones left the Stones and was replaced with guitarist Mick Taylor. (Many people think Jones died and then was replaced, because he died a month later and the Stones weren't in the public view with Taylor joining the band until after Jones's death in July, 1969). In December, 1974, Mick Taylor left the Stones and was replaced by Ron Wood, Wood joining the band in March/April, 1975.

When was Rolling Stones Records formed?

It was formed in March of 1971, and the first record out was *Brian Jones Presents The Pipes of Pan of Joujouka*, posthumously.

What groups are on Rolling Stones Records?

Rolling Stones Records artists were: Kracker in 1973, Howlin' Wolf, Peter Tosh, and Brian Jones.

Who has recorded with The Rolling Stones?

Guests in Stones' sessions are not too common, but people that have been in the studio with them, and were recorded with the band, are:

Lennon and McCartney — *We Love You*

Al Kooper — *You Can't Always Get What You Want*

Gene Pitney — *Little By Little*

Graham Nash — *Little By Little*

Peter Townshend — *Slave*

Dave Mason — *Street Fighting Man*

Who has played onstage with The Rolling Stones in concert?

The Stones are not known for having surprise guests appear, but a few are: Eric Clapton, Doug Kershaw, Sugar Blue, Mick Taylor (after he left the Stones), Carlos Santana, Tina Turner, Elton John, Chuck Leavell, Linda Ronstadt, Stevie Wonder, and a few others.

Have the Stones ever recorded with other name people?

Although sometimes not being credited for being on the record, the members of The Rolling Stones have playing with various people, among the following:

Mick Jagger sings on: *Da Doo Ron Ron* with Andrew Loog Oldham in 1964

You're So Vain with Carly Simon

Don't Look Back with Peter Tosh

Heart of Stone with Neon Leon

Ron Wood's album, *I've Got My Own Album To Do*

The Beatles' *All You Need Is Love*

Keith Richards: Keith played on L.P.'s by:

Black Uhuru

Peter Tosh

Max Romeo

Marianne Faithful

Brian Jones: Brian played on the Beatles' *Baby You're A Rich Man* and *You Know My Name Look Up The Number*.

Bill Wyman: Bill played on *Howlin' Wolf's London Sessions* and with Turkey Buzzard.

Charlie Watts: Charlie played with Alexis Korner's Blues Incorporated, and Rocket 88.

Why do The Rolling Stones record in different countries?

Studios, engineers, and location are major factors in terms of recording. The Stones like places and people they seem to mix well with, and use studios that offer equipment that may not be commonly found at other studios, equipment that would fit the sound they are looking for.

When have The Rolling Stones toured Europe?

They first played in Europe in 1964, then in 1965, 1966, 1967, 1970, 1971 (British tour only), 1973, 1976 and 1982.

What is the biggest concert The Rolling Stones ever gave?

The largest was their concert at Altamont on December 6, 1969, where some 500,000 people saw the Stones perform the last show of the 1969 U.S. tour.

How long does it take for the Stones to get a tour together?

By the time the Stones announce that they will go on tour, which usually begins the month after the announcement is made, over six months of tour preparations have already been in progress. First, a preferred time of year to tour (fall, winter, spring, or summer) must be decided, and then the venues have to be booked. Big venues require at least six to eight months advance booking. Financial backers must be obtained to help finance the road expenses. Posters and tour books are printed weeks in advance, and the band rehearses for about eight to ten weeks before the start of the tour. Most of the hard work is already done before the tours are even announced.

Cologne, Germany

THE AUTHORS

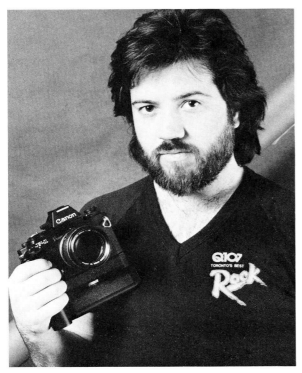

Philip Kamin was born in Toronto on February 20, 1955, and makes this city his home. A graduate of Ryerson Polytechnical Institute, he picked up a camera for the first time in 1978 and went on the Genesis tour. His work met with instant success, and since then his photographs have appeared world-wide in magazines, songbooks, programs, publicity campaigns, and a book, and on album covers and posters. In addition to Genesis, Kamin has photographed The Rolling Stones, The Who, Peter Gabriel, Cars, Phil Collins, The Police, Rush, Led Zeppelin, Van Halen, Black Sabbath, Rod Stewart, Triumph, Ian Hunter, Teenage Head, Martha And The Muffins, Roxy Music, Ian Drury.

Kamin's first book, co-authored by Peter Goddard is titled *The Rolling Stones Live* (in the U.S., *The Rolling Stones: The Last Tour*).

Philip Kamin uses Canon cameras and equipment exclusively: F1 and A1 bodies with motor drive; lenses: 24mm f/2, 35mm f/2, 50mm f/1.4, 85mm f/1.8, 135mm f/2, 200mm f/2.8, and 300mm f/4 Aspherical, and Canon strobe system.

James Karnbach was born in Brooklyn, New York. He has worked on three books: *The Rolling Stones: The First Twenty Years, The Book of Rock Lists,* and *Rock Almanac.* Karnbach has also contributed to a number of feature films, videos, TV and radio specials — *Heroes of Rock'n'Roll, The Complete Beatles* (The Beatles), *The Kids are Alright* (The Who), *One for the Road* (The Kinks), *Let's Spend the Night Together* (The Rolling Stones), *The Wizard of Waushaka* (Les Paul), *It Came from Hollywood, When the Music's Over, Girl Groups, The Rolling Stones Past and Present.*